How Long Is Long?
Comparing Animals

Vic Parker

Heinemann
LIBRARY

Chicago, Illinois

www.heinemannraintree.com
Visit our website to find out more information about Heinemann-Raintree books.

To order:

☎ Phone 888-454-2279

🖥 Visit www.heinemannraintree.com to browse our catalog and order online.

© 2011 Heinemann Library
an imprint of Capstone Global Library, LLC
Chicago, Illinois

Edited by Nancy Dickmann, Rebecca Rissman, and Sian Smith
Designed by Victoria Allen
Picture research by Hannah Taylor
Original illustrations © Capstone Global Library Ltd
Original illustrations by Victoria Allen
Production by Victoria Fitzgerald
Originated by Dot Gradations Ltd
Printed and bound in China by South China Printing Company Ltd

14 13 12 11 10
10 9 8 7 6 5 4 3 2 1

Library of Congress Cataloging-in-Publication Data
Parker, Victoria.
  How long is long?:comparing animals / Vic Parker.
    p. cm.—(Measuring and comparing)
  Includes bibliographical references and index.
  ISBN 978-1-4329-3958-8 (hc)—ISBN 978-1-4329-3966-3 (pb) 1. Length measurement—Juvenile literature. 2. Body size—Juvenile literature. I. Title.
  QC102 .P367 2011
  530.8/1 —dc22   2010000930

Acknowledgments
The author and publisher are grateful to the following for permission to reproduce copyright material: Alamy Images pp. **4** (© vario images GmbH & Co.KG), **7** (© Juniors Bildarchiv), **10** (© Hornbil Images); © Capstone Publishers pp. **5, 26, 27** (Karon Dubke); Corbis pp. **6** (DLILLC), **18** (Momatiuk); FLPA p. **24** (Minden Pictures/ Flip Nicklin); istockphoto pp. **8** (© Fusun Genc), **14** (© youding xie); naturepl.com pp. **12** (Gabriel Rojo), **16** (Andy Rouse); Photolibrary pp. **20** (Dea/ C. Dani-I. Jeske), **22** (M. Krishnan).

Photographs used to create silhouettes: istockphoto, squirrel (© Laurence Dean); shutterstock, foot (© andrisr), rat (© basel101658), peacock (© Vule), tiger (© gaga), crocodile/ whale (© Svetlana Eltsova).

Cover photograph of a male Ebony Jewelwing damselfly reproduced with permission of Photolibrary (Don Johnston).

Contents

Words appearing in the text in bold, like this,
are explained in the glossary.

What Is Length?

The length of something is how long it is from end to end. Some things, such as railroad tracks, are long. Other things, such as trains, are shorter.

Trains are made up of cars. Longer trains have more cars.

4

To measure length you can use a ruler or a tape measure. These are marked in inches (in.) and feet (ft.).

Using a tape measure is sometimes easier with two people.

Long Animals

Some animals are longer than others. Being long helps some animals to move fast. For example, a dolphin has a long body. Water glides over it smoothly. This helps it speed along.

Bottlenose dolphins can be 6½ to 13 feet long.

Other animals are long because they have long tails. Long tails can be useful. They can help animals to balance or to grip things. They can also be used to **communicate**.

A long-tailed macaque's tail is even longer than its body.

How Long Are Your Feet?

Have you ever measured how long your feet are? **Compared** to a younger brother's or sister's feet, your feet might be very long. But how long is long?

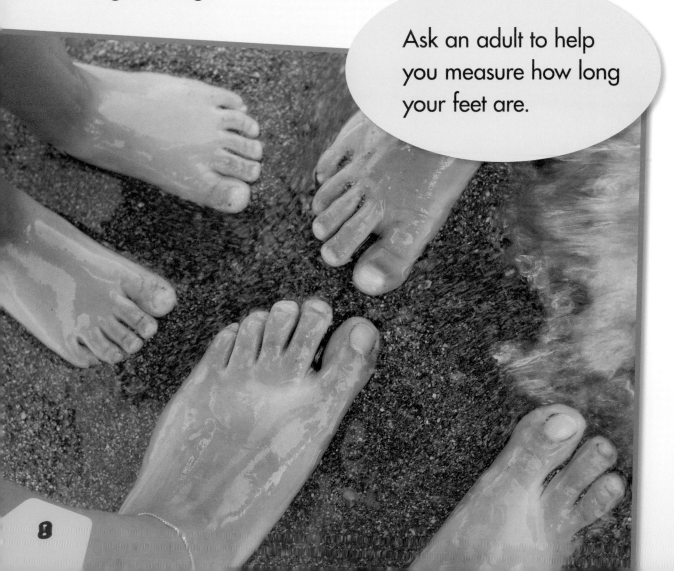

Ask an adult to help you measure how long your feet are.

A black rat can be 16 inches from the tip of its nose to the end of its tail. A black rat like this would probably be more than twice as long as your foot.

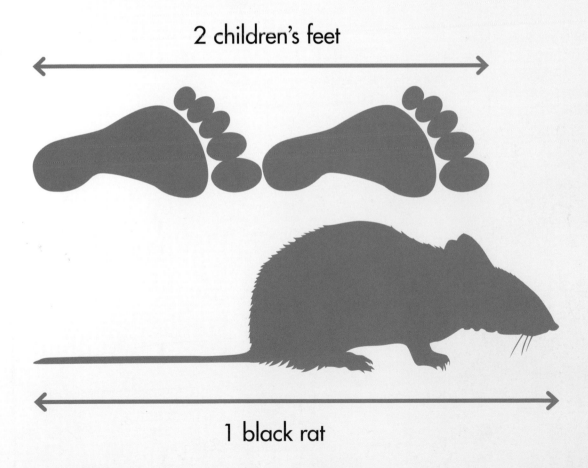

2 children's feet

1 black rat

What is longer than a black rat? ➡

Indian Giant Squirrel

A squirrel can be longer than a black rat.
The largest type of squirrel is the Indian giant
squirrel. It lives in tall trees in **Asia**.

Squirrels are **rodents**,
like mice and rats.

Indian giant squirrels can grow to be over 36 inches long. If you put two black rats end to end, an Indian giant squirrel would still be longer.

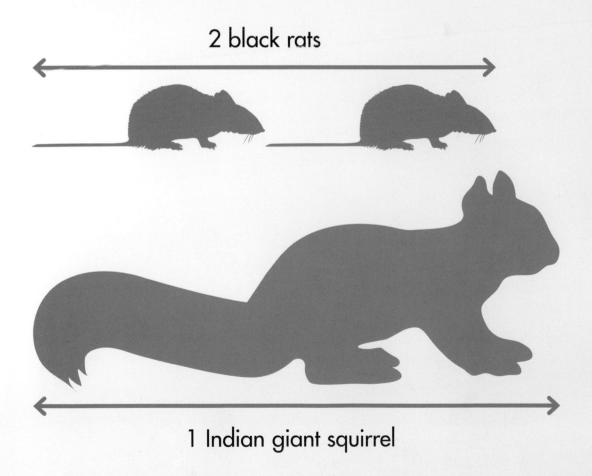

2 black rats

1 Indian giant squirrel

What is longer than a giant squirrel? ➡

Giant Armadillo

A giant armadillo is longer than an Indian giant squirrel. Giant armadillos live in forests in South America. They eat **termites** and ants, and sometimes mice and rats.

A giant armadillo has a shell made from overlapping bony scales.

A giant armadillo can measure 5 feet long. This means that a giant armadillo is more than one and a half times as long as an Indian giant squirrel.

Remember!
12 in. =1 ft.

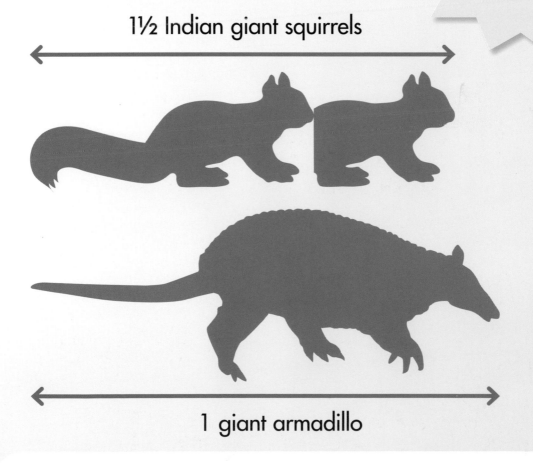

1½ Indian giant squirrels

1 giant armadillo

What is longer than a giant armadillo? ➡

Peacock

A peacock can be longer than an armadillo. Peacocks have long, beautiful tails, called trains. A peacock raises its train to display its stunning feathers.

It can be hard for peacocks to fly when they have such long tails.

A peacock can be about 10 feet from the tip of its beak to the end of its train. It would take two giant armadillos to be as long as a peacock.

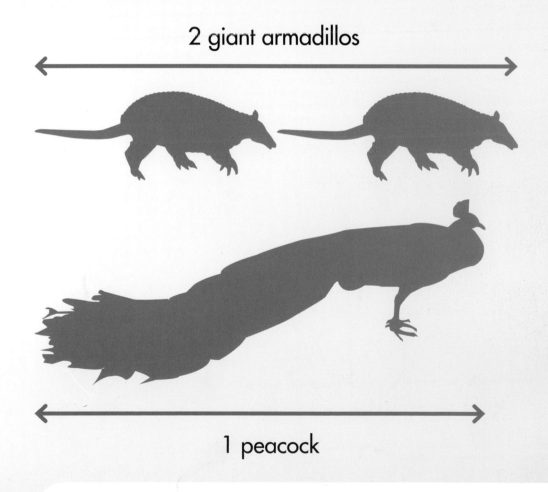

2 giant armadillos

1 peacock

What is longer than a peacock? ➡ 15

Tiger

A tiger is longer than a peacock. Tigers are the longest of all the big cats—they are even longer than lions. Male tigers are longer than female tigers.

Most tigers have over 100 stripes.

A male tiger can measure up to 13 feet long. This is nearly one and a half times as long as a peacock.

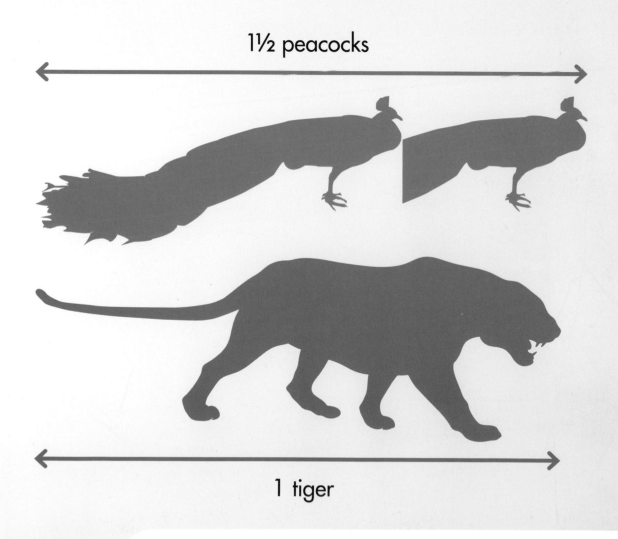

1½ peacocks

1 tiger

What is longer than a tiger? ➡

Southern Elephant Seal

A Southern elephant seal is longer than a tiger. These animals are called elephant seals because the males have long noses. They use their nose to make a loud roaring noise.

Male Southern elephant seals are called bulls. Females are called cows.

A bull Southern elephant seal can be 16½ feet long. This is 3½ feet longer than a tiger.

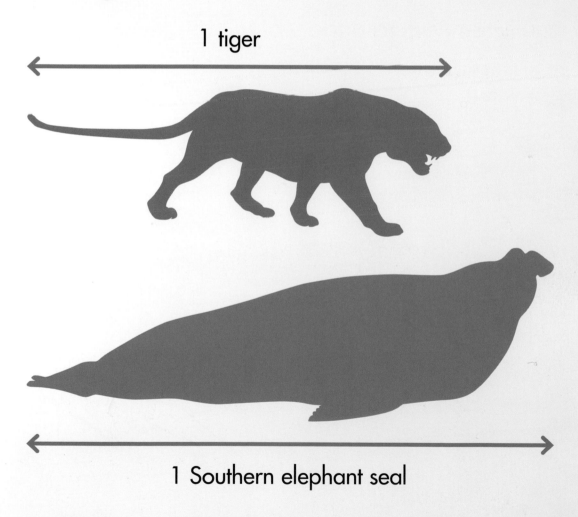

1 tiger

1 Southern elephant seal

What is longer than a seal? ➡

Saltwater Crocodile

A saltwater crocodile is longer than a seal. Many saltwater crocodiles live in Northern Australia. They eat animals of all sizes, from small monkeys to huge water buffalo.

Saltwater crocodiles can go for months without catching food.

A male saltwater crocodile can be 20 feet long—sometimes even more. This is longer than a Southern elephant seal and an Indian giant squirrel lined up together.

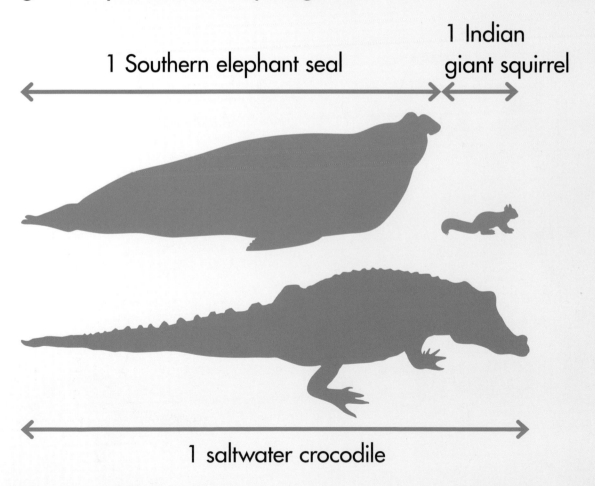

1 Southern elephant seal

1 Indian giant squirrel

1 saltwater crocodile

What is longer than a crocodile? ➡

Python

A python can be longer than a saltwater crocodile. The longest pythons are found in Southeast **Asia**. They live in forests and **grasslands** near water. They are good swimmers.

Pythons use their long bodies to wrap around things and grip them tightly.

Pythons are the longest of all snakes. They can be 33 feet long. This is nearly as long as two saltwater crocodiles laid nose to tail.

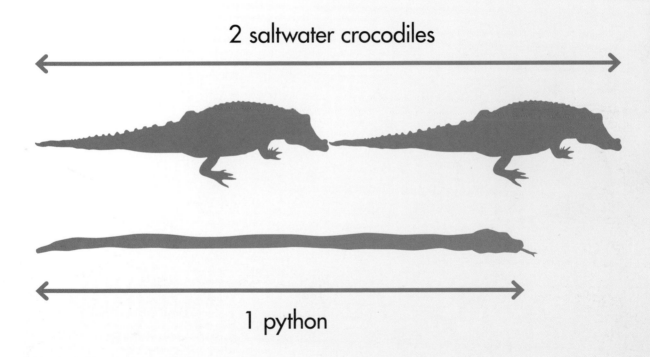

2 saltwater crocodiles

1 python

What is longer than a python? ➡

Blue Whale

A blue whale is longer than a python. Blue whales live in the oceans, but they are not fish. They are **mammals**. This means that they feed their babies milk.

A blue whale breathes when it surfaces, using a blowhole on the top of its head.

Blue whales are bigger than any other animal. They can be almost 100 feet long. This is as long as three pythons stretched out end to end, or 75 black rats!

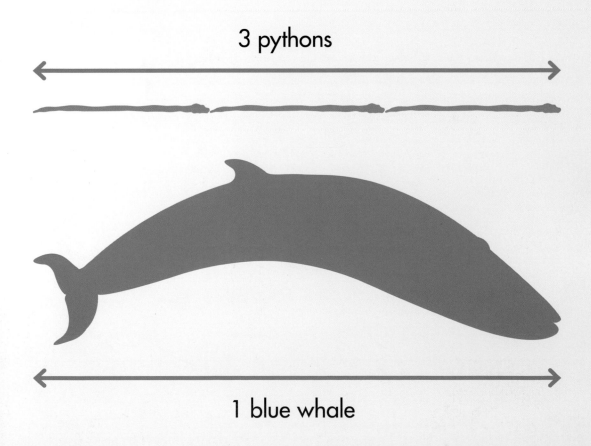

3 pythons

1 blue whale

Measuring Activity

Things you will need: a helper, scissors, a tape measure, masking tape, paper, a pencil, different colored ribbons, and long objects that you can measure, such as a tennis racket, a scarf, an umbrella, and a table.

1. Work together to cut a piece of ribbon to the same length as your first object.

2. Stretch out the ribbon against the tape measure and measure how long it is in inches.

3) Stick the ribbon on the top of a large piece of paper. Write down the name of the object you measured and how long it is in inches.

4) Do the same with other long objects, using a different colored ribbon for each one.

5) Stick the start of each new ribbon right below the last one. This will make it easier to **compare** how long the objects are.

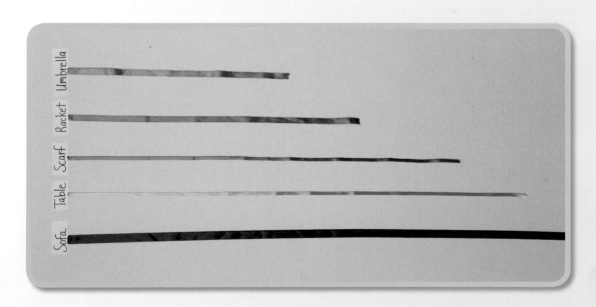

Find out: Which object on your chart is the longest?

Long Quiz and Facts

Small lengths are measured in inches (in.).
Larger lengths are measured in feet (ft.).

Quiz

1. What unit would you use to measure the length of a mouse?

   a) inches b) feet

2. What unit would you use to measure the length of a cat?

   a) inches b) feet

3. What unit would you use to measure the length of a shark?

   a) inches b) feet

Answers: 1 =a   2 =a   3 =b

Long Facts

- A hawk moth's tongue can be up to 12 inches long! It uses this long tongue to feed from tall flowers.

- A man named Melvin Boothe has the world's longest fingernails. They measure about 30 feet long!

- The Australian pelican is the bird with the longest beak. Its beak can grow up to 18½ inches long.

- The world's longest bus is 82 feet long and can hold 300 passengers.

- A giraffe's neck can be about 6½ feet long.

- The Amazonian giant centipede can be up to 12 inches long. It eats bats, mice, and spiders.

- The longest type of lizard in the world is the Komodo dragon. Many are about 6½ to 10 feet long!

Glossary

Asia large part of the world that includes the countries of India, Pakistan, Bangladesh, China, Japan, Indonesia, and Thailand

communicate to give information to someone else. This might be done through making sounds or talking, by writing, or by using parts of the body to make signs.

compare to look at two or more things and see how they are the same and how they are different

grassland area where grass and grass-like plants are the main plants that grow

mammal creature that is warm-blooded and that feeds milk to its young

rodent small, furry animal with large teeth. Mice, rats, and rabbits are rodents.

termite insect that eats wood and looks similar to an ant

Find Out More

Books

Fandangleman, Rupert. *Comparing Creatures*. Chicago: Heinemann Library, 2010.

Hewitt, Sally. *How Big Is It? (Measuring)*. North Mankato, MN: Stargazer, 2008.

Hirschmann, Kris. *Is a Paw a Foot?: All About Measurement*. (Artlist Collection: The Dog). New York: Scholastic, 2005.

Web Sites

www.funbrain.com/measure/

Try this simple quiz, which asks you to identify the correct measurements in inches.

www.cdfa.ca.gov/dms/kidspage/KidsIndex.htm

Find out more about measurement through the facts and activities offered on this website.

Index